Brody, Lucie and the Food Fairy

written by
Claudia Lemay, RD

illustrated by
Chris Hamilton

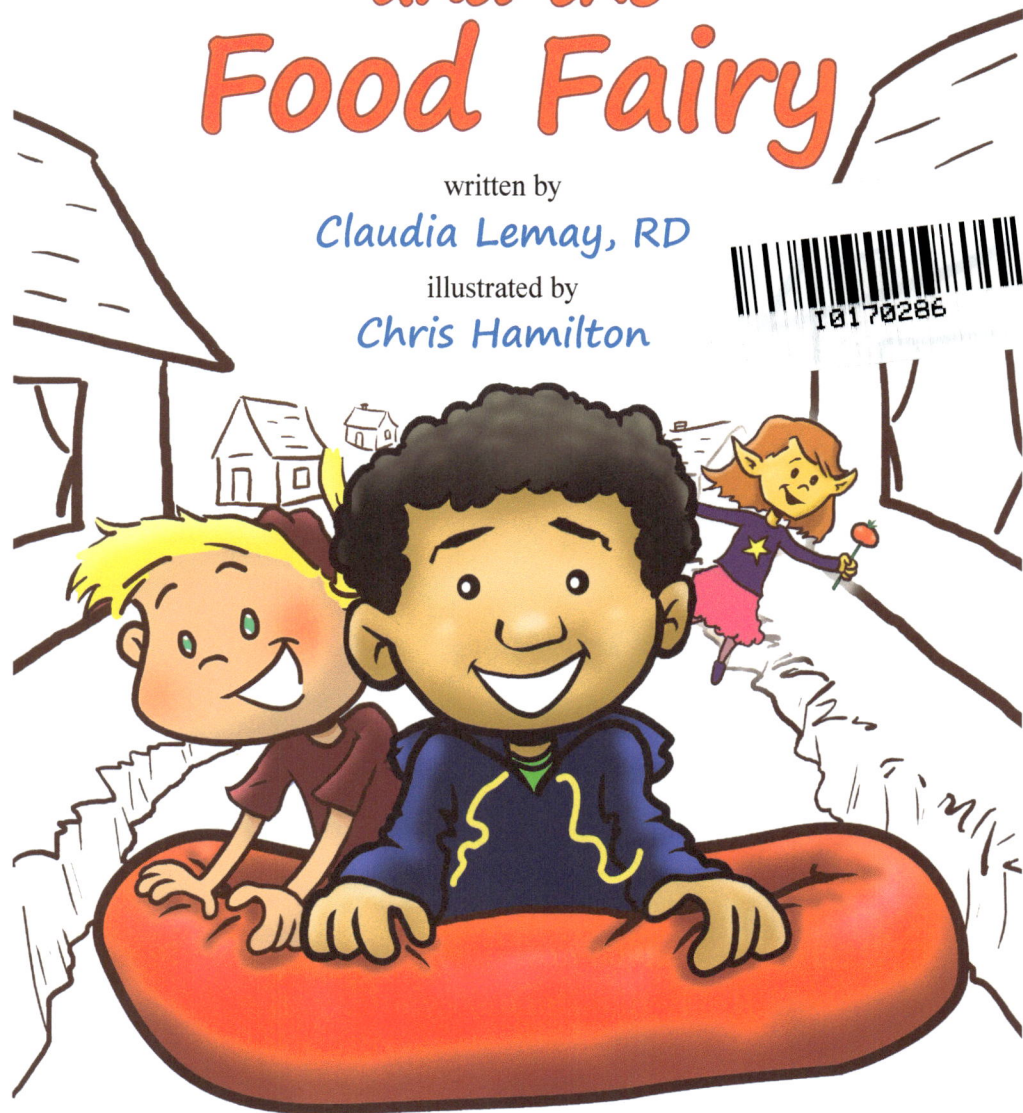

An exciting adventure to explain
type-1 diabetes to children.

When Lucie arrived at school, she went looking for her best friend Brody like she did everyday. But she could not find him anywhere. Lucie usually found Brody sitting on the monkey bars, swinging from the monkey bars or hanging from the monkey bars. But not today!

Lucie walked over to the football field wondering where Brody had gone, when a schoolmate pointed over to the street and said: "Are you looking for Brody? I think that's him over there."

Lucie saw Brody sitting down on the curb, looking very, very sad. Brody never looked sad! She ran over to him. "Hey! What's going on?" she asked. But Brody did not respond.

"What's the matter?" she asked, kneeling down to get a better look at him.

"I don't feel well," he said, sounding upset. "I'm tired...hungry...thirsty...and I feel super drowsy! Plus, everything looks all blurry!"

Lucie was surprised. She had never seen her friend behaving like this.

She opened her bag and grabbed her water bottle. "Do you want some?" she asked.

He shook his head and replied, "I drank two bottles already."

"Well, I'm taking you to the nurse, whether you like it or not," she said as she pulled him up. As he stood, he let out a huge, heavy sigh. They walked together hand in hand to the school in silence.

The school receptionist took one look at Brody and decided to bring both children to the nurse's office straight away.

"I hope you feel better soon, Brody!" she said as they walked in.

"Well, hello there, Brody!" said the nurse. What's going on?"

"Hi Ray, I don't feel well," replied Brody in a weak voice. "Oh, by the way, this is my best friend Lucie."

"Nice to finally meet you, Lucie!" He turned to Brody: "Should we check your blood sugar?"

"No...well...maybe...yeah, probably..." stammered Brody.

"Huh? You two know each other?" interrupted Lucie, her mouth open in surprise.

Neither Brody nor Ray answered Lucie's question. Instead, with a serious look on his face, Ray stretched out his hand and said: "Glucometer please, and go wash your hands." Brody washed his hands at the sink and returned quickly.

Brody lifted his shirt and opened a little red pouch that was hidden underneath. He pulled out three pieces of fancy-looking equipment that Lucie didn't recognize. He gave all three to Ray. Ray pushed a button on the first piece and it beeped. He then pricked Brody's finger with the second piece that had a needle, and they all heard a "click."

Brody squeezed his finger and a small red droplet appeared. Lucie shrieked, pale-faced.

"Is that b-b-blood?"

"Yes, it's blood, but it doesn't hurt, not too much, anyway. I do it all the time. This is how we'll know if my blood sugar level is too high...or too low."

"You have sugar in your blood? How come? How did it get there?"

Ray was too busy to answer. He dipped the white tape sticking out from the third piece of equipment into the blood droplet.

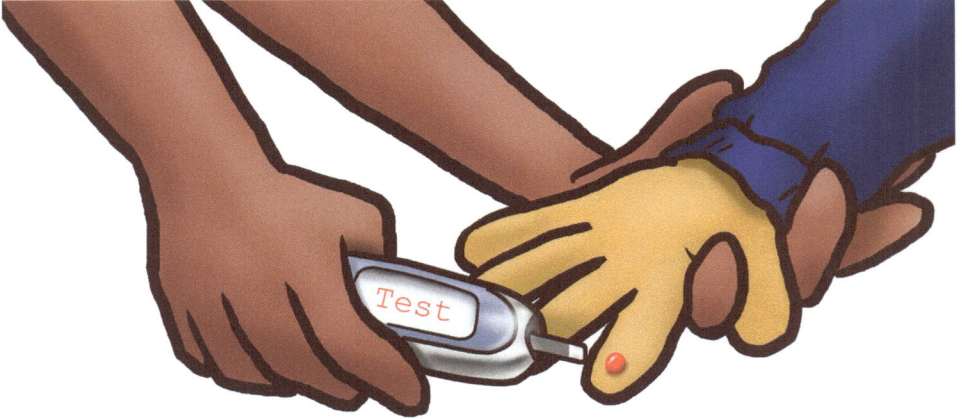

"Wow, no wonder you are feeling lousy! Your blood sugar is sky-high! Do you have any idea how it got so high?"

"Uh...I may have eaten one chocolate bar my friend gave me on the bus...or maybe two... as well as my break-fast," answered Brody, sheepishly.

"Ah! Okay, let me help you with your pump and then I'll go call your Dad."

Lucie was burning to ask many more questions, but chose to remain quiet this time, waiting for the right moment.

"Can Lucie stay here while you talk to my Dad?" Brody asked.

"Sure!" answered Ray with a smile as he finished pushing buttons on Brody's pump. "There, you should feel better soon."

Ray left the room to call Brody's Dad while the kids sat together. He came back shortly and announced: "Since your Dad was running errands nearby, he has decided to come see you. I suggest that while we wait for him, I explain diabetes to Lucie. It seems like she has a lot of questions so I am guessing you never told her about your disease? And since you let her come in with you, I am also guessing you are now ready to have her know?"

Ray was looking at Brody, but Brody was intently looking at his feet. His shoes sure seemed interesting!

Brody eventually looked up at Ray, who nodded encouragingly. Brody nodded his head and turned to Lucie again and said in a small voice: "I have diabetes."

"You have what? Dyer-dee-dees? What's that? Is that bad? Are you sick?" Lucie blurted out, suddenly worried.

"Di-a-be-tes," pronounced Ray clearly. "It's quite common but also quite serious, and it happens when the pancreas doesn't work properly. Here is the pancreas," Ray added, pointing to a yellow thing on a poster.

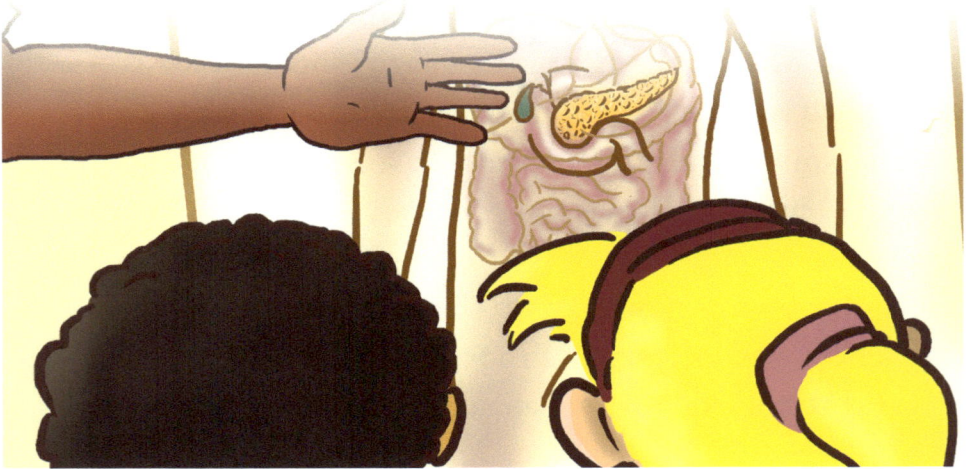

"Let me start at the beginning. When we eat food, carbohydrates from the food we eat get into our stomach, where they are broken down into sugar during digestion. The sugar then gets absorbed into the blood. Once in the blood, insulin allows sugar to enter the body's cells for energy. In people with diabetes, the pancreas does not make insulin. Without insulin, sugar from the food Brody eats cannot enter his cells, and builds up in his blood instead. Understand?" The two kids nodded so Ray went on.

"Sugar and carbohydrates are found in many foods like cereal, fruit, vegetables, yogurt, even candy. You know that sugar provides energy, right? No sugar, no energy. That's why he's not feeling well."

"Oh! What can we do?" Lucie gasped.

"Luckily, we have ways to get sugar into his cells," Ray answered. "Hey, I have an idea!

I know someone who is fantastic at explaining this kind of stuff," he said, smiling. "See you later!" he added and walked out.

Lucie and Brody barely had time to exchange puzzled looks before they heard a "swoosh" coming from the window...

A small creature with pointy ears had come flying into the office on a rainbow.

"Stargold! What are you doing here? I am so happy to see you! How are you? Did you come to visit me again?"

"Whoa, Lucie! That's a lot of questions. You haven't changed one bit! Hi, Brody!" she replied, giggling.

"Uhh..h-hello," said Brody shyly, trying not to stare. "Nice to meet you."

"Do you know who I am?" asked Stargold.

"Well, yeah!" said Brody, feeling better already.
"Lucie told me all about you and Growland zillions of times!
She told me how everyone has a house growing in Growland,
and how each house is someone's body in reality. I know
that I have to eat certain foods to provide materials for
Elves who are building my house, I mean my body, in
Growland!

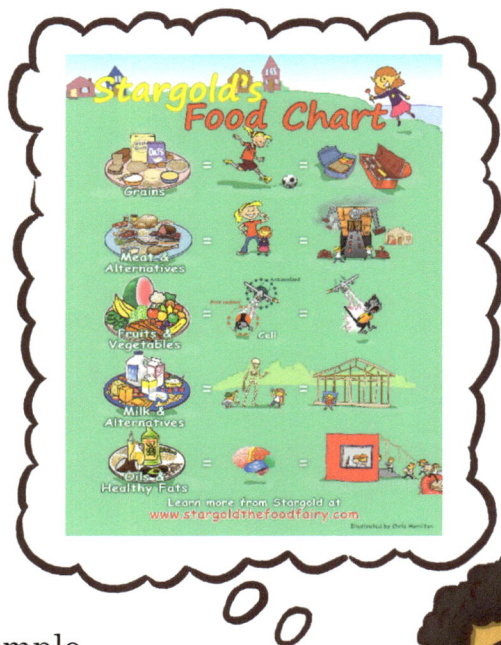

So, for example,
when I eat 'Protein Foods',
my Elves get bricks to build
the walls of my house, and
when I eat 'Whole Grains'
my Elves get energy and tools to work."

"Wow! Your understanding is phenomenal! But,
because of your diabetes, your case is a little different, or
rather, special..."

"But I don't want to be different OR special!" protested Brody, furiously.

"Well, everyone is different! That makes being different very normal. It's just that your Elves need a little extra help. Come to Growland with Lucie and I, and I will show you everything!"

She held out her hand and smiled, waiting for his reply. Lucie looked pleadingly at Brody. While hopping from one foot to the other, she added: "Please please please?"

Brody sighed, "All right then, let's go, otherwise I'll be hearing about this for the next 20 years."

Lucie took one of Brody's hands and Stargold grabbed the other, and up into the sky they flew. They flew over oceans and deserts, waterfalls and jungles.

Finally, they soared over a giant forest and arrived in Growland.

Brody's mouth stretched into a wide smile when he saw the thousands of rivers, thousands of tiny red boats and thousands of brightly coloured houses, all beautiful in their own way.

"As you can see, Brody, there are only rivers instead of roads in Growland. So we will be travelling by boat," Stargold declared.

Once they landed, they quickly hopped on a boat and started their journey. Stargold continued: "As you mentioned before, Brody, these houses are magical because each one represents someone's body."

She suddenly clapped her hands and said: "Look! There's Lucie's house!"

Lucie's house was bigger and taller than the last time they had visited. Lucie recalled with fondness just how magical and amazing her house truly was. She waved at her Elves to thank them and they waved back.

"I want to see my house too!" said Brody.

"Of course! It's right over there," Stargold pointed across the river, and as the two kids looked on, she added in a more serious tone: "There it is."

Right away, they noticed there was something odd about his house: there were tons and tons of unopened lunchboxes surrounding it. There were so many that they completely blocked the path to the house from the river.

They also noticed that none of Brody's Bodybuilder Elves were working. Some were even sleeping!

"Why aren't they working?" asked Brody, angrily. "Don't they have jobs to do?"

"Yes," said Stargold, "but they don't have the energy to do their work."

"Why don't they eat food from the lunchboxes, then? That will give them energy!" sputtered Brody impatiently.

"Your lunchboxes are locked. The Elves usually open the lunchboxes with a key called insulin. Your pancreas doesn't make insulin, so your Elves can't open them."

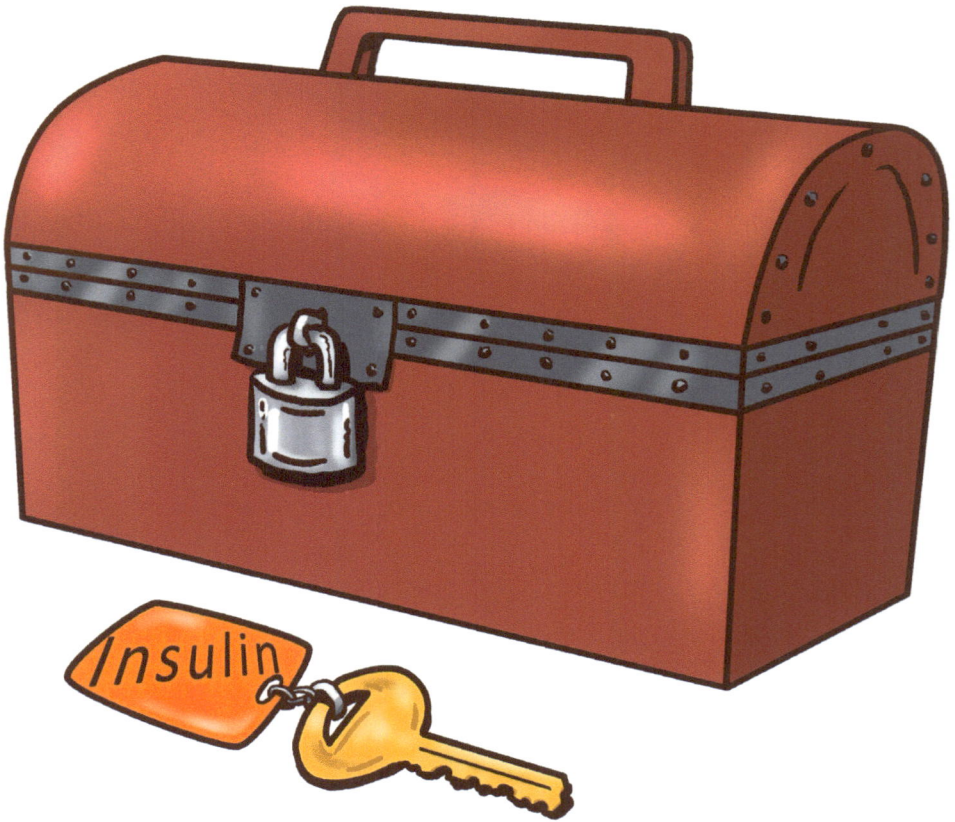

"When the rivers are blocked," Stargold went on, "many of the materials can't get through and this place becomes chaos. The Mayhem Monkeys love chaos, so they are more likely to show up and cause damage."

"We have to do something! But what?" exclaimed Lucie.

"We need to bring some insulin keys to Brody's Elves quickly," Stargold said, "but we won't find any here. Let's visit the Endocrine Queen. Her kingdom is very important and she is the only one who can help us."

"Where can we find her?" asked Brody.

"She is on Langerhans Island, in the Pancreatic region. Let's fly there - this boat is way too slow!"

Stargold grabbed Brody's hand, Brody grabbed Lucie's, and up into the sky they flew again. Soon after, they landed on a tiny egg-shaped island, surrounded by many other similar-looking islands.

"The Endocrine Queen lives up there!" Stargold said, pointing to a castle on top of a hill.

As they neared the castle, Stargold added: "The Queen is very important. We must make this visit brief."

The large glass castle doors opened before them, as if the visitors had been expected.

"Greetings, Brody, Lucie, and Stargold. I have been waiting for you," said the Endocrine Queen regally.

"Huh? How come?" asked Lucie.

"You have?" said Brody, almost at the same time. "Ms. Queen, can you please tell me why people have diabetes?"

"What's it like to be a queen? Do you have servants? How many?" added Lucie.

"Hmm, so many questions at once..." said the Queen, unfazed.

"Let me start by saying that indeed, I was expecting you. My specialized nerve cells announced your arrival."

"Cells? You mean like cell phones?" asked Brody, his eyes wide.

The queen chuckled, the kids having managed to make her laugh. "Yes, just like cell phones, I suppose. Secondly," she continued in more serious tone, "it is not known what causes diabetes exactly. In any case, you will need to acquire the insulin keys on your own. You will find them in a chest located in the uppermost room of the North Tower. Choose the chest labelled 'Beta,' not the one labelled 'Alpha.' Also, be sure to take only twelve keys. Twelve… and not one more." She cautioned. "Now, if you'll excuse me, I need to attend to the messengers of my kingdom at all times, in order to control my affairs properly."

"Thank you very much, Your Majesty," she said to the Queen, bowing respectfully.

"Yes, thank you Ms. Queen," said Lucie and Brody, as they attempted to bow as well.

"I know where the stairs to the North Tower are. Let's go!" Stargold said.

They ran to the end of the hall, passed the kitchens, library, two dining rooms, and finally came to a long, twisty flight of stairs. They climbed it two at time and found themselves at the top of the tower, in a dimly lit circular room.

Lucie, who had walked to the far end of the room, called out: "Look! There are two chests here!"

Brody ran over and noticed the word 'Beta' engraved on one of the chests. "This is the one!" he exclaimed. "It's exactly how she said it would be!" He lifted the heavy lid and found hundreds of insulin keys inside.

"Hooray! I am going to be okay!" he said excitedly.

"Remember to only take what you need, though," emphasized Stargold.

"Why? There are so many keys in here! I could take all of them and be fixed forever! I could be 'normal' like you and Lucie!" said Brody.

"It does not work that way! You should follow the Queen's directions. She said only twelve keys," insisted Stargold.

"I don't care! I don't want to be different anymore!" said Brody, filling his pockets with keys while Stargold looked on disapprovingly. "Here, Lucie, take some too!"

Lucie reluctantly held out her hands, not wanting to disappoint her friend. They stuffed their pockets with keys until they overflowed. Then, the three of them flew back to his house in silence.

As soon as they arrived, Lucie and Brody started distributing the keys to the Bodybuilder Elves. The Elves woke up, unlocked the lunchboxes with their keys and began eating, relieved.

"Thank you, Brody and Lucie!" They cheered. "We feel great!"

They were cheerful until every single lunchbox was unlocked and every single morsel of food eaten. They were so happy! Until...

There were no lunchboxes left at all. That's when they started feeling tired again. Really tired. One Elf sat down, and then another, and another. Suddenly, Brody felt tired too. And angry.

"Now we are all tired and hungry again. Ow! I have a headache! I shouldn't have given them all those keys!" yelled Brody, kicking at the empty lunchboxes. Lucie came closer.

"Brody! You are all shaky and sweaty!" she said, alarmed.

Stargold intervened. "It's okay, Lucie. Brody is experiencing 'hypoglycemia' because the amount of sugar in his blood is too low. It will pass soon. When this happens," she added, "Brody's mom calls him 'the low-sugar monster,' to make him laugh. Don't be upset, Brody. Now you know not to use too much insulin at once. Here, let me help you."

26

Stargold waved her wand and a tray magically appeared with a variety of juice, candy and soda.

"These contain just enough sugar to make you feel better," Stargold explained. "Drink some juice or eat 6 candies, you will see."

"What? CANDY?!" interrupted Lucie. "That doesn't provide any tools, just energy!"

Stargold laughed. "We need to give him sugar right now and candy is perfect for that because the sugar gets absorbed into his blood quickly."

"This is kind of awesome, you know," said Lucie, ogling the candy.

Brody took a small sip of juice and grabbed 18 candies. He ate 6, placed 6 in his pocket for later and gave the rest to Lucie, who immediately stuffed them in her mouth.

"Wait! Those still have the wrappers on them!" said Stargold, chuckling.

They all started laughing and Brody started to feel a little better.

They walked over to a tree and sat down on its grassy base, still giggling.

Once she was finished eating her candies, Lucie said to Brody: "I get it now! That thing that you have under your shirt..."

"You mean my insulin pump?"

"Right. It works just like the keys!"

"Well, yeah, I guess it does..." said Brody.

"Since your body doesn't make insulin, it has to come from somewhere else.

Here, we were able to bring some to your Elves. But at home, the insulin comes from the pump. That's what Ray was doing when he was pushing all those buttons."

"Yes. He was making sure I was getting the right amount of insulin."

"Ha! Cool!"

Since Brody still looked a bit sad, Stargold added gently: "I know you want to be like other kids, Brody, I understand that. Sometimes I wish I was a normal kid like you and Lucie, and not an Elf..."

"Being an Elf is cool." Brody protested, "Diabetes is not cool and it makes me embarrassed and mad. It's so unfair!"

"Is that why you didn't tell me about your diabetes before?" asked Lucie.

"Yeah, I thought you wouldn't want to be my friend anymore."

"Brody, why wouldn't I want to be your friend because of something like that? That's silly! You always ask me how my day is going, and you actually listen to the answer! You make me laugh. You let me play video games on your computer. Everyone loves you because you are nice, and you care about people!"

She paused, opening her hand that was still full of candy wrappers, and joked, "but the real reason we are friends is because you give me candy!" They laughed.

"Seriously though, Brody. You are an awesome guy. If I didn't want to be your friend because of your diabetes, what kind of person would that make me?"

"I guess I never thought of it that way," he replied.

"It's not your fault that your Elves can't open their lunchboxes, Brody. It's not even their fault," added Stargold. "It is what it is! Everyone is born with something special and different, and everyone has unfair things happen to them. We are all normal and special at the same time. Furthermore, you are learning that it's not that difficult to be loved and accepted after all. All you have to do is to love others first! If you understand this now, at your age, you are already way ahead of many adults. And all this learning is happening because of your diabetes. So, it's not all bad, is it?"

31

Brody felt relieved. "How lucky I am to have friends like you two!"

"Well, I think that's my cue to bring you both back!" said Stargold, smiling at him.

They all shared a hug and then flew back over the giant forest, jungles and waterfalls, deserts and oceans, and finally through Ray's window into the school.

"This is it then, Stargold? We won't see you for a while?" asked Lucie, sad to have to say goodbye again.

"Yes, it may be a while Lucie, unless you get into trouble, of course," she winked. "I will miss you guys. You are both awesome."

With that, she swooshed away out the window, leaving behind only her sparkling rainbow. Brody's dad walked in with Ray just as Stargold's last sparkle dissipated into the air. When Brody saw his father, he yelled, "Dad! I have the most amazing story to tell you!"

The End

Stargold's Tips

1. Eat meals at regular times.

2. Keep carbohydrate choices consistent to help control your blood sugars.

3. When filling your plate, mostly choose the following:

   - Fresh Fruits and Vegetables
   - Whole Grains
   - Beans and Legumes
   - Nuts and Seeds
   - Healthy Oils (olive, flax seed, walnut, hemp, canola, etc.)

4. Don't Forget To:

   - Read food labels
   - Drink lots of water
   - Eat together with friends and family
   - Go play outside!

Stargold's Pyramid

Mediterranean Diet

Illustrations by Chris Hamilton

At Brody's Table...

To order copies of the "15 Grams of Carbohydrates" in poster format visit www.stargoldthefoodfairy.com

37

Acknowledgements

- Thank you to Brody, my son Justin's friend. Brody is the inspiration behind this story. One day after school, Justin told me all about Brody who has "dyer-dee-dees." The real Brody is a curly-haired, very wise little boy who is very accepting of his disease. The "Angry Brody" was just for the purpose of creating a story.

- Thank you to Brody's parents Theo and Ailsa for sharing their experience.

- Thank you to the real Elves of BC Children's Hospital who help so many children and their families to better understand, cope, and manage their diabetes. They graciously accepted to help me make this story as medically accurate and authentic as possible: Alexandra Yule, RD, Jill Middlemiss, RD, CDE, Deep Chhina, RN, CDE.

- Thank you to Chris Hamilton for making my stories look totally awesome.

- Thank you to Doug McKinnon for his expertise with those frustrating computers, his graphic-design talent and his uber patience with my 22 million last-minute changes.

- Thank you to Jamie Oliver for his advocacy on teaching nutrition to kids and kicking me into action. He is my own hero.

- Thank you to my kids, Justin and Amélie. Without them, there would be no Stargold (and I would have a lot more time to myself to eat "bonbons" and relax once in a while).

- Thank you most of all to my husband Peter Zakrzewski, for his support and encouragement in all my "I have a fantastic new idea!!!" moments.

Claudia Lemay, RD
Author

Claudia Lemay is a dietitian and author who resides in Surrey, British Columbia, Canada, where she works as a clinical dietitian and lives with her husband, two kids and many pets. She is also the author of "Stargold the Food Fairy," a children's book about nutrition.

To learn more about Lucie, Brody, the Food Fairy and healthy nutrition for children, or to order Stargold's educational tools and books, please visit: www.stargoldthefoodfairy.com.

www.ingramcontent.com/pod-product-compliance
Lightning Source LLC
Chambersburg PA
CBHW041817040426

42452CB00001B/6